JESUS IN LUKE'S GOSPEL

Michael Trainor

JESUS IN LUKE'S GOSPEL

ST PAULS

Acknowledgment:
Unless otherwise indicated, the scripture quotations contained herein are adapted from the *New Revised Standard Version* of the Bible, copyright, 1989, by the Division of Christian Education of the National Council of Churches of Christ in the United States of America, and are used by permission. All rights reserved.

JESUS IN LUKE'S GOSPEL

First published August, 1995

National Library of Australia
Cataloguing-in-Publication Data:
Trainor, Michael
Jesus in Luke's Gospel
1. Jesus Christ. 2. Bible. N.T. Luke – Criticism, interpretation, etc. I. Title.
(Series: Australian biblical project; 1)
ISBN 1 875570 54 3
226.406

Cover design: Bruno Colombari SSP

Published by
ST PAULS – Society of St Paul,
60-70 Broughton Road – (PO Box 230) – Homebush, NSW 2140

ST PAULS is an activity of the Priests and Brothers of the Society of St Paul who proclaim the Gospel through the media of social communication.

Contents

For St Patrick's Catholic Community,
Mansfield Park,
South Australia

The Australian Biblical Project

The difficulties of life can lead us to look for different ways to make sense of what is happening to us. The earliest faith communities have tried to make sense of their times in the light of their experience of God and Jesus. Their conviction of God's involvement in the midst of life's perplexity is reflected in the writings of the Bible. These writings can also help us find meaning in what is happening around us. Their insights can help us live authentically. As we seek to grapple with the complexity of the social and ethical issues of our time, the faith perspectives offered us by the Bible's writers about God and Jesus are a powerful source of wisdom.

This task of engaging the faith perspective of these ancient writers can seem daunting. Understanding the Bible, its history or even the tools that scholars use in coming to a deeper appreciation of its various forms of literature can overwhelm us.

The *Australian Biblical Project* presents the best of current biblical scholarship in a way that enables readers to come to a deeper appreciation of the Bible. The *Project* is explicitly designed for people with little background knowledge to the Bible who are seeking to engage the

Scriptures in the light of our contemporary world. The *Project* seeks to address two fundamental questions:

- How relevant is the Bible today?
- What might it say to the situations in which we find ourselves?

Writers of the *Project* communicate the insights of biblical scholarship effectively and are drawn from the various Christian traditions. Therefore, while the *Project* is based on fine critical biblical scholarship, it is fundamentally ecumenical and will make the Bible accessible to all.

The series of books which make up the *Project* cover various aspects of the Old and New Testament. These books may be used for private reflection or as the basis for prayer and study in small faith groups, Bible study groups, house churches and basic Christian communities.

The chapters of each book offer material suitable for a session of study and reflection in a small group setting. A book's chapter could form the basis for group sharing which would benefit from individual or private reading and reflection prior to the meeting.

Questions conclude each chapter. These questions are critical. They bring the Bible into dialogue with our own world and our own experience. They are the catalyst for group discussion or individual reflection. Through them the contemporary implications of the material presented can be teased out.

It is hoped that the *Australian Biblical Project* will make an important contribution to the faith life of the Christian churches in our land, that it will help to take the dust-covered Bible off our shelves, and that it will show what relevance this ancient and nurturing collection of sacred writings has for us today.

Michael Trainor
Series Editor

Suggestions for group use

1. Read the material of the chapter prior to meeting.
2. Decide on the length of time the group wishes to meet and stick to it. If hospitality is offered (a cup of coffee, biscuits, etc.) keep it simple.
3. As the group moves into the formality of meeting, participants could briefly recall what stayed with them from the last session.
4. Some time (though not an excessive amount) might be given over to identifying essential points that people noted in their reading. A brief time could be spent helping to clarify perplexing insights.
5. A question such as 'What *touched* you as you read?' rather than 'What did you *think* about the chapter?' might be a better way to open up reflection on the chapter.
6. The group leader would need to check that (4) does not dominate meeting time and that group sharing does not turn into a debate over the chapter's content.
7. The questions at the end of each chapter are the heart of the meeting and where most time would be spent.
8. These questions are intended as a guide and not to be slavishly adhered to. Not all questions need to be covered either. In fact, the questions may suggest others more pertinent to the group.
9. Before the meeting concludes:
    - decide on who will co-ordinate the group next time. Rotating group leadership helps to take the responsibility off one person;

- invite each person to review how they found the session. This is intended as a review of the meeting and not another chance to continue the discussion.

A suggested meeting structure *(90 mins)*

1. Welcome *(5 mins)*
2. What stayed with you from the last meeting? *(10 mins)*
3. What important points did you note from reading the chapter? What *touched* you as you read? *(15 mins)*
4. Work through questions from the chapter and/or other questions suggested by the group *(50 mins)*
5. For next time: Who leads the group?
6. Review of the meeting *(5 mins)*

A check list for the session leader

1. Going overtime can be a source of frustration for people, so ensure the group sticks to its agreed time for meeting.
2. It helps the flow of the session if the leader is familiar with the suggested outline and time sequence of the meeting agreed upon by the group.
3. Members of the group will find sessions far more enjoyable if everyone participates. At times it may be necessary to quieten those who seem to be doing the most talking and encourage those who are much quieter.
4. It can become a trap if the leader is expected to be the group's encyclopaedia rather than its facilitator. It may help to check out this expectation when assigning leadership for the session and to encourage members to share their own wisdom rather than look to one particular person.
5. It is important for the group to keep moving through each session rather than getting bogged down on what might be a rather technical point. If this happens suggest someone research the point in contention, for example, and bring the information to the next meeting.
6. Be a time keeper. Remind the group of how much time is left until the end of the session. This helps to keep the group focused.
7. If the questions at the end of each chapter seem suitable and helpful, make sure that appropriate time is set aside to work through them.
8. At the end of each session organise the co-ordinator for next time. Spread the work load!

Foreword

On the wall close to the little table where I tap out these words through a keyboard on to a computer screen hangs a copy of an eleventh century Greek mosaic. I bought it years ago as a poster, mounted it and it has continued to journey with me ever since.

The mosaic seems to be part of a much larger work. It captures the faces of four people gazing beyond the frame of the mosaic into my room and world. Three of them are staring to the left in the direction in which the characters are moving. They seem apprehensive or saddened. One of them, the younger of the three, has his face turned downwards.

In the midst of the three is a fourth countenance turned to the right and looking back from the direction they have all journeyed. The face is serious, but not frightened. It is searching.

The face belongs to St Luke.

The mosaic has always attracted me. I see it is a microcosm of my own religious quest. The three faces turned in the direction of the journey seek to anticipate what awaits them. They steel themselves for some unprepared crisis.

They desire to know how to deal with the unforeseen. Fear looms because of the possibility of being unable to control the unexpected.

The fourth face, that of Luke, is looking back. It looks back not to deny the possibility of failure and pain as part of the journey but as recognition that the way to deal with the future is by honouring the past. Wisdom is a gift from generations that have gone before.

The artist of this eleventh century mosaic has captured something essential about the task of the Gospel writer. Luke stands in the midst of a terrified community, looking back to remember the story of the tradition which has enabled this community to journey forward. The story and the tradition is about Jesus and the first community of disciples. Luke draws strength from this vision which the artist recognises is able to provide encouragement to those journeying forward and feel perplexed, frightened and saddened by future possibilities.

In this book I have tried to capture something of Luke's conviction about Jesus and why he is essential for our journey into history. More than ever, Luke's Jesus offers us hope and power as we seek to grapple with some of the most perplexing and distressing issues never before imagined by human beings. Luke's Jesus is at the heart of this quest for meaning and wisdom in the midst of life's issues. I am grateful for many who have accompanied me in this quest and, specifically, those who have been with me in the writing of this book.

Over the past few years I have had the privilege of sharing in the faith life of the members of the Roman Catholic community at St Patrick's, Mansfield Park, South Australia. As I read Luke's Gospel in the light of this experience I find striking parallels between the Gospel's 'original' audience (with all the difficulties associated in defining the 'original audience' which will be discussed in the next chapter) and this contemporary faith community. Its people have enabled me to appreciate freshly the portrait which Luke presents of Jesus. For me, St Patrick's is a mosaic of the Christian community in its journey through history.

The vitality and obvious hospitality in this gifted, multicultural faith community reflect the key qualities which Luke seeks to encourage in Gospel's readers. In conversation and friendship with the people of St Patrick's, including its pastoral co-ordinator, Catherine Seward RSM, through presiding at their liturgies and breaking open the Word in their midst, I have been able to experience the wise, festive, healing, prophetic, saving and human Jesus about whom this book reflects. In deep gratitude for what this community has shared with me and the way it has encouraged my ministry among them, I dedicate this book.

1

Introducing Luke's Gospel

I remember the first meeting of someone who was later to become a close friend. I felt a little awkward in this initial encounter. We were unfamiliar to each other and perhaps even a little wary. We were different in many ways, age, family histories, locale, cultural experiences and profession.

Over time we shared our backgrounds and learnt the reason for our differences. Eventually suspicion and unease gave way to trust and confidence. Openness was accompanied by a readiness to share and a willingness to listen. In this atmosphere friendship blossomed. Initial awkwardness and shyness developed into a long and lasting friendship.

Reading Luke's Gospel for the first time is like initiating a conversation with someone we would like to befriend. We come to this Gospel initially a little awkward and shy. Perhaps we do not know much about this Gospel which comes from a place, history and culture so different from our own.

The purpose of this book is to help in the process of befriending Luke's Gospel. This will be assisted by a number of predispositions toward reading the Gospel:

a desire to take the Gospel seriously;
an openness to allow it to address us from its own cultural setting;
a willingness to converse with it out of our own background.

When did it all begin?

The Gospel is a story about the life and teaching of Jesus. It is written well after the actual events it is describing, at a time when the Christian community is attempting to come to terms with its ongoing life in a new cultural setting.

Each of the four Gospels is written:

- *from* a unique faith perspective about Jesus;
- *for* a specific faith community;
- *with* a particular historical and cultural situation in mind.

The Gospels are serious documents of faith. They seek to make the story of Jesus accessible to a later group of believers as stories and sayings about Jesus were synthesised, adapted, expanded and edited. These believers are chronologically and culturally distant from the historical Jesus.

It is well accepted that the Gospels went through *three stages* in the process of their formation.

The *first stage* is identified with the actual ministry of Jesus who adapted his preaching about the reign of God to the images familiar to his audience.

The *second stage* in the process of Gospel formation occurred with the preaching about Jesus by his first disciples*. Through their preaching they helped to establish communities of disciples by shaping their message of Jesus according to the circumstances of their communities. Imagery and expression which were originally Jewish, for example, were culturally adapted for a non-Jewish audience.

With the death of these initial preachers the communities they founded recognised a need to commit to writing their memory of the words* and deeds of Jesus. In this *third and final stage* in the formation of the Gospel the story of Jesus is adapted in the light of the circumstances of the

* An asterisk indicates that further information about the term or expression marked by the asterisk is provided in the glossary.

audience addressed by each of the Gospels.

When we come to read Luke's Gospel, we are reading a document that has gone through these three stages of formation. Fundamentalist Christians would argue that the Gospels are literal stories of what actually happened. This approach suggests the Gospels are almost like a journalist's account of the actual events frozen by the Gospel text.

The position taken in this book is different. When we read Luke's Gospel we are reading it at this *third stage* of formation. Just as Jesus adapted and shaped what he said and did according to the needs of his audience (first stage), so too did the first preachers about Jesus (second stage) and the evangelists on the death of the community's founding preachers (third stage).

How old is Luke's Gospel and what was Luke's community like?

The writer of Luke's Gospel used *three sources* in composing the Gospel.

The *first* was the Gospel of Mark which was already in circulation (and written around 70CE, of the 'common era'*, the period of history common to Jews and Christians, traditionally referred to as 'AD'). Luke follows generally Mark's story line, with significant expansions, omissions and alterations.

A *second source* of material is suggested by comparing the Gospels of Luke and Matthew. They share 220 verses of sayings of Jesus not present in Mark's Gospel. This second source scholars call 'Q' (from the first word of the German *Quelle*, meaning 'source').

A *third source* of material were traditions about Jesus

unique to Luke's own community. By working with these three sources, the author of what we call the *Gospel according to Luke* sought to formulate a fresh narrative about Jesus for new pastoral situations never previously envisaged either by Jesus himself or the author of the Gospel of Mark.

Scholars are reluctant to identify definitively the cultural characteristics and pastoral concerns of Luke's intended audience. This reluctance stems from an inability to know the Gospel's 'original audience' or actual writer.

The Third Gospel* was anonymous and its authorship accredited to Paul's companion 'Luke' only in the late second or early third centuries. The designation of authorship to an anonymous writing (called 'pseudonymity') was a common literary practice of the period which gave heightened credibility to a document intended for a wider audience.

However, granting these reservations about accurately pinpointing the precise location for the writing of Luke-Acts, some reasonable assumptions can be made. These are suggested given the Mediterranean world in which these writings were created.

This can lead to a properly defined historical context. A careful reading of Luke's own writings also offers us a window into the Greco-Roman* world and helps to clarify the socio-political context in which the evangelist wrote.

Most biblical commentators would agree that Luke wrote the Gospel about fifty years after the death and resurrection of Jesus, around 85CE. In that time the Christian movement had spread beyond the land of Palestine, grown in membership and, true to the spirit of Jesus, crossed over those barriers that kept cultural groups separated.

Those who first formed the community of Jesus' disciples were Jewish peasants* drawn mainly, though not exclusively, from the northern part of Israel around Galilee. The vision offered, of a religious and social renewal inclusive of the most destitute and unholy, attracted followers. They saw evidence of this vision in Jesus' preaching and healings. His words and deeds confirmed for them that a time of renewal in holiness and peace had been inaugurated. They believed that through Jesus the vision of holiness which expressed the heart of authentic Judaism was being renewed. In Jesus, God was actively healing people, bringing wholeness or *shalom* to creation and calling Israel's political, economic and religious leaders back to the true spirit of the Law of Moses or Jewish Torah*.

The reign of God which Jesus preached and practised was reflected in the Greco-Roman world of the first century in his community of disciples. The community grew and spread north into Syria and Asia Minor, west into Greece and Italy and south into Africa. This movement around the Mediterranean meant that later followers of Jesus came less from a Jewish background and more from the Gentile* world. However, even this distinction of Jew and Gentile, needs to be more carefully nuanced. For there were many in Jesus' day, and definitely more in Luke's time, who were from Jewish parentage and were at home in the Gentile or Greco-Roman world. Historically, this occurred because of Alexander* the Great's conquest of the Middle East.

How did the Christianity survive outside its Jewish roots?

As time went on, a variety of people from different cultures became part of this renewal which began with Jesus and his community of disciples. How did a religious movement, whose origins were purely Jewish, survive for later generations of different cultural and social background?

This was the great question which Luke sought to answer, and did so in two ways.

First, Luke offered a new portrait of Jesus which would address itself to a generation of Christians, who were predominantly Gentile, seeking to live in a world never experienced by the Jewish Jesus. This new story of Jesus was presented in what is called 'the Gospel according to Luke'. Through the Gospel and the story of Jesus, Luke presented a portrait of a faithful God, still faithful to the promises made to Israel and now, in Luke's day, to the Gentiles and all who felt excluded from God's life.

Second, the evangelist also wrote a second volume, called 'the Acts of the Apostles', which offered a fresh interpretation of the story about the origins of the Christian movement. This story illustrated that the action of a God who was faithful to Israel and Jesus was also faithful to the community of disciples in history, including Luke's community.

The growth of the Christian community beyond the borders of Israel was a legitimate and divinely inspired development. This development was authenticated by God, especially through the action of the Spirit and the Spirit-empowered preaching of the Twelve*, the Seven* and Paul.

The strong narrative and theological connection between the two stories, of Jesus in the Gospel and the early Christians in the Acts of the Apostles, is illustrated by their literary structure*:

Gospel	*Book of Acts*
1:1-4 Prologue*	1:1-5 Prologue
1:5-3:38 Birth Story of Jesus	1:6-26 Birth Story of the Church
4:1-13 Preparation by the Spirit for Mission	2:1-13 Preparation by the Spirit for Mission
4:14-9:50 Ministry in Galilee	2:14-12:25 Ministry in Jerusalem, Judea, Samaria
9:51-19:27 Jesus' Journey to Jerusalem	13:1-28:16 Paul's Journey to Rome
19:28-24:53 Ministry in Jerusalem	28:17-31 Ministry in Rome

The parallel outline of both volumes is as much a statement about theology* as it is about literature. It is a statement about God's involvement in human activity. According to Luke, the story of Jesus is incomplete without the story of the early Christian communities and, by inference, the story of the audience addressed by these stories; Jesus' ministry is a model for the ministry of the Christian community; the story of the Christian community is grounded in and parallels the story of Jesus.

Through writing these theological histories or stories the evangelist addresses several questions:

1. How do Jesus' followers live authentically in new cultural and social situations while trying to remain faithful to the original spirit and vision of Jesus?
2. Can the point in history which Luke's community has arrived at in following Jesus, be considered reliable? Can it be trusted?
3. How do Jewish and non-Jewish followers of Jesus live in harmony with each other, while respecting their respective traditions?
4. What are the implications of Jewish and non-Jewish Christians breaking bread at the same table of the Lord?

Luke's Gospel addresses a vibrant, active, missionary-conscious Christian community seeking to deal with problems on two fronts: internally, with issues of multi-culturalism, wealth, table communion, ministerial effect-iveness and diversity; and externally, with relationships and the wider Greco-Roman society.

Faced with these issues Luke was left with one of two options: to encourage Gospel readers to retreat into their own sectarian vacuum cut off from the reality of life around them, or encourage them to engage the questions and issues of their world. Luke chose the second option.

The Gospel and the Acts of the Apostles reflect that choice. Simply put, in both volumes Luke encourages readers to remain in dialogue with their world while bringing the tradition that they had received about Jesus to bear on it.

In writing the Gospel, Luke already had Mark's Gospel from which to work. Just as Mark had adapted, refashioned, expanded and generally reshaped stories inherited about Jesus for a Roman rural audience in the 70s, Luke did the same for a Greek, urban audience of the mid-80s. This audience was made up of people who were mainly from the non-elite* sector of society, though there was a growing number who were elite*. Luke's community comprised both rich and poor, some Jews but predominantly Gentiles. The evangelist reshaped Mark's Gospel adding other material about Jesus which had been told to Luke's community by its founding preachers. The result was a fresh Gospel designed to encourage later followers of Jesus as they endeavoured to adapt as a community to new social situations.

Besides retelling the story of Jesus' first followers and how they dealt with difficult situations, Luke also offered a fresh, rich and colourful portrait of Jesus. What follows presents some of the main insights about Jesus that come through the Gospel and are relevant today. Luke's presentation of Jesus is profound. The following is by no means exhaustive but seeks to explore some of the main threads of Jesus' portrait as found in the Gospel. Among other images, Luke presented Jesus as wisdom figure, prophet*, saviour, healer, dinner host and guest, innocent martyr, and 'the human one'. In the chapters ahead we will explore each portrait in turn. The approach used to explore these images, while essentially thematic, will crisscross through the Gospel and offer a way of reading Luke's Gospel by means of its unique presentation of Jesus.

Reflecting on Luke's Gospel from our cultural background

These images presented in the Gospel were relevant for Luke's community. They spoke powerfully to the current pastoral situation experienced and offered a way of making the story of Jesus applicable to a later period of history.

Luke's process, of adapting the story of Jesus to make it suit another time and culture, needs to be continued in our day. As we seek to address the most pressing questions of our age, questions dealing with community life and the survival of our planet, the process which Luke used becomes more pertinent. By engaging in a meaningful and ongoing conversation with Luke's Gospel, the portrait of Jesus which Luke offers can speak freshly to our day offering us encouragement, hope and direction.

True friendship occurs when both partners are equally respected and neither dominates the relationship. In practice this means that while there is a time when we remain silent and allow Luke's Gospel to speak to us from its own unique historical and cultural setting, there also comes an important moment when we too speak.

For our friendship and appreciation of Luke's Gospel to grow there is a time when we must also acknowledge our own real questions and allow those to enter into the conversation. The questions at the end of each chapter are designed to allow this to happen. These questions are only a guide and may suggest others that are more relevant.

Finally, a glossary of frequently occurring terms with which readers might not be familiar is found at the back. These terms are indicated by an asterisk '*' in the text when they first appear.

Before moving on to the next chapter, a reading of the whole Gospel in a couple of sittings using the literary outline suggested above might be helpful. Such a comprehensive reading gives a feeling for Luke's overall structure and story of Jesus, which the following chapters will explore in greater depth.

As we begin to befriend Luke's Gospel through its portrait of Jesus, we allow it to address us from the first century Greco-Roman setting. As we converse with the Gospel taking into consideration our own questions and concerns, a new and deep appreciation of the Gospel will develop. Initial shyness and awkwardness will give way to a long-lasting friendship.

QUESTIONS

1. As you begin this reflection on Luke's portrait of Jesus, what do you hope will become clearer for you?
2. What do you consider are the pressing questions or social issues to which people are looking for answers?
3. When people think of their world, how relevant do they see the Gospels in speaking to it?
4. What do you think keeps people today from reflecting deeply on Jesus?

2

Jesus: wisdom figure

Ilona is a single parent who has struggled throughout her whole life with relationships, with her parents, her friends and, more recently, in her marriage. She has a seven-year-old son. What she most desires now is to know how to live a good life that will bring happiness to herself and her son.

She would like to communicate to her son those values which she believes will make him truly happy and from which he can learn. At the heart of Ilona's journey in life is her search for *wisdom*.

Luke writes the Gospel for a people who are searching for wisdom. In the opening four verses of the Gospel (Lk 1:1-4), we find a very brief summary of the evangelist's purpose for writing.

> [1]Since many have undertaken to set down an orderly account of the events that have been fulfilled among us,
>
> [2]just as they were handed on to us by those who from the beginning were eyewitnesses and servants of the word,
>
> [3]I too decided, after investigating everything carefully from the very first, to write an orderly account for you, most excellent Theophilus,
>
> [4]so that you may know the truth concerning the things about which you have been instructed (1:1-4).

According to this introduction, sometimes called the 'prologue', Luke respects what previous writers and Gospel proclaimers have done in communicating the tradition about Jesus.

Luke intends to 'write an orderly account' so that the Gospel's readers might know 'the truth' (1:4) about what they have been instructed. This will be built on the efforts of those who were eyewitnesses to the ministry of Jesus and became 'servants of the word' (1:2).

What is translated as 'the truth' in verse 4 is a Greek expression '*asphaleia*' which means 'assurance' or 'certainty'. Luke's purpose in writing is to reassure the Gospel's intended audience as it struggles in its journey. In other words, Luke is concerned about enabling Gospel readers to identify the *wisdom* in their search and in the catechesis* or faith education in which they have been involved.

The wisdom tradition

Wisdom in Luke's day was essential for full living. It was the search to know God within the ordinary experiences of life. These experiences became the basis for wisdom in which God was revealed.

The tradition which had developed about wisdom in the Hebrew Bible* was a deeply profound one. In the collection of writings concerned with wisdom in the Old Testament, called 'Wisdom Literature', wisdom is recognised to be with God from the very dawn of creation (Prov 8:25-26). The universe is an expression of God's wisdom (Wis 8:24) which is also encapsulated in the Torah, the first five books of the Jewish Bible.

Wisdom is from God, like God, personified God and often called 'Lady Wisdom' (Wis 6:8; Sir 24). She emanates from God and is discovered in the learnt experiences of human beings over the ages. The insights from Lady Wisdom could also be communicated through the community's sages.

Writers and philosophers of the Greek world considered wisdom as a gift of the gods which only the privileged could enjoy. The Jewish Scriptures* on the other hand recognised wisdom as God's gift available to all who would search for her.

Jesus Luke's wisdom figure

Jesus himself would have absorbed this Jewish appreciation of wisdom. For the writers of the Christian community, Jesus was seen as a source of wisdom. Like wisdom herself, he was from God and revealed God. The appreciation about wisdom inherited from the Old Testament and circulating in the Greco-Roman world affected the evangelist's portrait of Jesus in the Gospel.

Luke's Gospel and the Book of Acts could be considered as the evangelist's response to the readers' search for wisdom within circumstances that made them feel distant from the origins of their faith. The Gospel and Acts concerned Jesus, the first community of disciples that gathered around him and the way this community was able to move beyond its original Jewish culture into the Greek-Roman world.

In the Gospel, Luke pursues this concern about the search for wisdom by presenting Jesus as the wisdom figure. He is presented as the one to whom people with questions about life are invited to come. This was a fresh way of looking at Jesus.

As Luke introduces the reader to this portrait, the opening chapters are important. These stories are unique in all the Gospels. Mark's Gospel begins with the preaching of John the Baptist, the baptism and temptation of Jesus and then moves into his public ministry.

Luke begins with two carefully constructed chapters presenting us with the stories surrounding Jesus' birth and infancy, before picking up Mark's beginning in chapter 3 with the preaching of John the Baptist. These chapters offer us a highly compressed theological picture of Jesus. The infancy story is not concerned with biographical informa tion about Jesus but with Luke's *appreciation* or theology of him, who he is for the Gospel's hearers/readers. The birth story, while based on history, is concerned more with theology than with historical accuracy.

Luke's story of the birth of Jesus

The Gospel writer has designed these first chapters by placing the birth story of Jesus alongside that of John the Baptist. The two are paralleled. This technique focuses on and provides emphasis for the annunication of Jesus' birth and circumcision. While John the Baptist, for example, is *wondrously* born to an elderly couple, Jesus is *miraculously* born to a couple who have not lived together.

Luke's point is clear: the circumstances surrounding Jesus' birth emphasise that it is a divine event; Jesus' birth is God's act and Jesus is from God; he is 'Son of the Most High' and heir to King David (Lk 1:32); he is 'Son of God' and king (Lk 1:35,32).

To a Gospel audience steeped in the Hebrew Scriptures, all these images which Luke employs to speak of Jesus are packed with a meaning which taps deeply into its memory of Israelite history.

According to Luke, in the birth of this child is summed up Israel's history and the realisation of its dreams. In Jesus is found the source of true wisdom for which Luke's readers are searching within their own time. This aspect of Luke's portrait of Jesus as a source of wisdom introduced in the birth story subtly continues into the rest of the Gospel, reaching its concluding expression in Jesus' death and resurrection. The first hint of this wisdom theme occurs at the *place* where Jesus is laid after his birth.

The place of Jesus' birth

Since our childhood the Christmas crib has been used to teach us, among other things, that Jesus was born in a stable (perhaps because of the lack of hospitality of some grumpy innkeeper!). A careful look at the Gospels reveal that Luke says nothing about a stable and in Matthew's Gospel Jesus is found (by the Magi) in a house.

In case the reader might overlook it, Luke mentions three times that Jesus is laid 'in a manger' (2:7,12,16), a feeding trough for animals.

> And she gave birth to her firstborn son and wrapped him in bands of cloth, and laid him in a *manger*, because there was no place for them in the inn (2:7).

Luke emphasises two points here with this preoccupation on the manger:

(1) Jesus is the food that nourishes a people.

(2) He is also wrapped in 'bands of cloth'.

Luke's audience could also identify this with the birth of King Solomon, the royal and ancient figure of Israelite wisdom. In the Book of Wisdom, Solomon declares 'I was nursed with care in [bands of cloth]. For no king has had a different beginning of existence' (Wis 7:4-5).

Jesus, like Solomon, is nursed in bands of cloth. Like Solomon, he is a true source of wisdom to whom Luke's readers are invited to come and be nourished (see Proverbs 9:1-3,5).

It is to this wisdom, once the exclusive possession of the royal and specially chosen, that shepherds are first drawn. An angel speaks of a sign which is *for them*: 'a child wrapped in bands of cloth and lying in a manger' (2:12).

The shepherds

The angelic appearance to shepherds (2:8-14) serves more than simply informing a wider, poorer audience about the event in the manger. Shepherds were considered by some as sinners. They were regarded as thieves who used the property of others for sheep grazing.

The angelic announcement of this sign intended *for them*, for the shepherds themselves, reminds the reader that the search for wisdom belongs also to those who are excluded from society. According to Luke, the unholy are especially invited to draw close to God's wisdom present in Jesus.

The infancy story concludes with the familiar scene of Jesus in the temple sitting among the teachers in conversation with them (Lk 2:41-51). This story is framed by two statements about Jesus' wisdom:

> The child grew and became strong, *filled with wisdom*; and the favour of God was upon him (2:40).
>
> And Jesus *increased in wisdom* and in years, and in divine and human favour (2:52).

Jesus, whose birth is presented as that of a wisdom figure, grows in wisdom during adolescence. Both references associate this growth in wisdom with the 'favour' (Greek: *charis*) or 'grace of God'. In other words Jesus' wisdom comes from God.

Other wisdom images in the Gospel

If we continue to trace Jesus' career through the Gospel it should not surprise us to find other references to his wisdom: when Jesus is criticised for his table companions with society's outcasts he tells his accusers that he is a child of wisdom. This vindicates his action because 'wisdom is vindicated by all her children' (7:35).

In response to religious lawyers who are reproached by him for their neglect of justice and authentic Torah action, Jesus interprets his prophetic speech condemning their actions as 'the Wisdom of God' (11:49).

Much of Jesus' teaching throughout his public ministry was in the form of parables*, teaching which emerged from an appreciation of wisdom which he absorbed. These parables, some of which we will look at in the next chapter, flowed from the wisdom out of which he lived. They came out of his own experience of God and true source of wisdom.

In Jesus' final act in his public ministry, his death, he is portrayed as the wise person of the Hebrew Scriptures. He dies declared innocent by Roman authorities (Pilate and a centurion), with forgiveness on his lips, totally faithful to God in the midst of his suffering (23:26-43).

The final words of Jesus before his death echo the disposition of the truly wise person in the Israelite tradition: someone who trusts God completely, despite being overwhelmed by pain and loneliness.

Echoes of Jesus' cry of trust, 'Father, into your hands I commend my spirit' (23:46), can be found in the Old Testament. This is similar to the praying person's grief found in the Psalms of Lament or the anguish of the suffering just one in the wisdom tradition (Wis 2:13,16,18; 5:5).

For Luke's readers this portrait of Jesus, as the wise one, would have offered them encouragement in their own search to know how to live within the social and cultural complexity in which they found themselves. Jesus is offered as the model for how to live with a sense of wisdom which is from God.

To Ilona, seeking wisdom for herself and her son, and to all who seek to discern how to live happily, Luke presents Jesus as the one who knows how to *be* in life. He is the one in whom searchers of wisdom will find 'assurance' (*aspheleia*). If one wants genuine and lasting wisdom, says Luke, look to Jesus.

QUESTIONS

1. What do you understand by 'wisdom'?
2. What prevents people today from really moving beyond the surface of life towards discovering genuine wisdom?
3. From your experience, what do you think is the 'wisdom' or truth about life for which people search? What is the wisdom for which you search?
4. How might Luke's portrait of Jesus as wisdom be helpful for people today?

3

Jesus: prophet

John works in a factory and is uneasy about the treatment some of his fellow workers are receiving from management. He knows he must say something. There is an urge within him to speak up, name what he thinks is happening and why he believes it is wrong. John also knows that what he says will make him unpopular and he will become ostracised.

There is a connection between what John seeks to do in his workplace and the image of Jesus in Luke's Gospel. Luke presents Jesus as one who has this deep 'urge' to speak the truth. Jesus is from God and is the *agent of God's word.* Jesus is God's prophet.

Jesus' 'word-deed'

From our experience we know that words can be powerful. Words strung together make up sentences and become the basis for communication. They can be identified and verified, and their meaning looked up in a dictionary. This is the stable or 'static' dimension of a word. To appreciate fully Luke's presentation of Jesus as prophet and agent of the word of God, we also need to understand another dimension to word which is sometimes overlooked.

'Word' can also be understood in a more active sense. As we have seen, 'word' is regarded as that which is uttered in communicating information. A 'word' also has a *dynamic* effect on people and the world. Words are precious, unretractable and powerful. What is uttered is also, in some mysterious way, *effective.* The 'word' once uttered is eternal. Words have the power to bring about the intention of their pronouncer. This dynamic, effective dimension of 'word' was appreciated by the Jewish people.

The first story in the Bible in the Book of Genesis reflects this appreciation of 'word': God speaks and this speech brings about creation. For this reason, what the Hebrews mean by 'word' is better translated as 'word-deed'.

The word was both intelligible (it could be understood) and dynamic (it was effective). To speak of Luke's Jesus as a prophet is to embrace this sophisticated and active appreciation of 'word' as 'word-deed' familiar to Luke.

Luke presents Jesus like one of the prophets in the Jewish Scriptures who is empowered by God's Spirit: his birth is the act of God's Spirit who comes upon Mary and 'overshadows' her (1:35). She conceives and bears Jesus, the fruit of the Spirit's action.

The powerful action of God's Spirit involved at birth continues as Jesus prepares to embark on his ministry. The Spirit comes upon him after his baptism while he is praying (3:21-22) and he hears God's words 'You are my son, the beloved; with you I am well pleased' (3:22).

In the next scene the Spirit leads him into the wilderness to confront and overcome the devil (4:1-12), and fills him with power as he returns to Galilee and begins his ministry (4:14-15).

Jesus' public ministry

The opening scenes of Jesus' public ministry (4:16-5:32) are climactic. They summarise what will unfold in his ministry. They also bring together Luke's appreciation of Jesus as the agent of God's word-deed. In the first scene, set in the synagogue at Nazareth (4:16-30), Jesus *speaks* God's word; in the scenes which follow he *acts* this word out (4:31-5:26).

In the Nazareth synagogue, Jews stands up to read and preach from a text of Isaiah. What Jesus selects to read can be seen as heralding the kind of ministry which will unfold in the rest of the Gospel.

> 'The Spirit of the Lord is upon me, because he has anointed me to bring good news to the poor. He has sent me to proclaim release to the captives and recovery of sight to the blind, to let the oppressed go free, to proclaim the year of the Lord's favor' (4:18-19).

Jesus is presented by Luke as anointed with the Spirit. Because of this prophetic and regal anointment the action of God proclaimed by Isaiah to the Israelite people is again tangibly revealed in the ministry of Jesus. Luke is keen to assert that the ministry of Jesus continues into Luke's own day. 'Today,' says Jesus to the Gospel audience, 'this scripture has been fulfilled in your hearing' (4:21). As God's anointed one and prophet, Jesus continues to offer salvation to the world. The Spirit empowers Jesus, as it did all the prophets in the Israelite tradition, to encounter and defeat evil and to proclaim the good news of God's presence.

At the final chapter of the Gospel two disciples on their way to Emmaus identify Jesus as 'a prophet mighty in deed and word before God and all the people' (24:19). The reader, looking back over the Gospel, can see how Jesus is a prophet by what he does and says. His miracles* and power to heal, his preaching and parables, 'prophesy' (literally, 'speak forth') the presence of God active in his ministry. What Jesus says and does embraces the two dimensions of 'word' and reflects the one prophetic ministry. His healings, which will be reflected on in the next chapter, are one expression of his prophetic ministry; parables are another.

Parables

The parables are like riddles which have the capacity to so tease their listeners that they become stunned or shocked into seeing reality with different eyes. The parables' listeners, if they are open enough to allow themselves to be captured by the parable, experience a new capacity to recognise God's mysterious action within the everyday and the present. The parables have the power to become the vehicle of God's reign acting in the lives of their listeners. In other words, they can 'grab' listeners attracted to the world which they represent. Through the parable's twist or riddle its listener sees undiscovered possibilities of God's reign in human affairs.

In his parable-making, Luke's Jesus draws mainly on rural images as ways of communicating something of the diversity, intimacy and surprise of God's presence to a peasant audience. Anything can become a metaphor of God's action in the world: seed planted in difficult terrain which eventually bursts forth into an abundant harvest (8:4-8); a household lamp on its stand (8:16-19); the kind deed of an enemy (10:25-37); a barren fig tree (13:6-9); a growing mustard seed (13:18-19); hospitality at a dinner party (14:7-12); a zealous shepherd looking for a lost sheep or a woman sweeping her house to discover the lost coin or an anxious father awaiting a wayward son's return (15: 3-32).

The parables from Luke's prophet, Jesus, can also affirm what is happening in life, no matter how difficult or painful this may be. Such parables assert that life is where one is meant to be. The long haul for the follower of Jesus rooted in the present is preferred to a pie-in-the-sky spirituality which looks for God solely in the future and beyond.

The parable of the 'ten pounds' (19:11-27)

Luke's parable of the ten pounds (19:11-27) is one parable which counteracts the temptation, in the light of Jesus' imminent coming, to regard suffering as something in the past.

In the parable a nobleman leaves his servants with ten pounds and instructs them, 'Do business with these until I come back' (19:13). On his return he summons three of his servants. The first two are praised and rewarded for their investment of the money entrusted to them. The third, instead of investing, wrapped the money in a piece of cloth and buried it. He gave back exactly what had been given to him, without interest. The servant is reprimanded and his money given to the one who earned the most, with the words '. . . to all those who have nothing, even what they have will be taken away' (19:26).

A usual reading of the parable seems to condone capitalism that seeks to encourage financial risk-taking for the sake of economic gain. Profiteering seems to be the most important social virtue; before it all else is worthless. In this interpretation, the first two servants are the favoured ones; they invest the money given to them, gain interest for their investment and are able to return all this back to the nobleman. They are rewarded for their economic astuteness.

In this context, the parable becomes interpreted as a teaching about the effort and spiritual investment which disciples must make in their following of Jesus and commitment to the reign of God. The reward and commendation given to the first two servants in the parable suggest that divine reward will be given only to those disciples whose commitment to God involves a certain risk-taking.

Whatever of the merits of this interpretation, in the ears of a first century peasant majority and the victims of an economic schema controlled by a wealthy minority, the parable would be heard and interpreted quite differently!

Peasant farmers in Jesus' day

In the agrarian world of Jesus' day, peasants were the victims of injustice in several ways. If they had retained original ownership of their family property exorbitant taxation on their crops gradually became burdensome to the point that they could not pay taxes. They found themselves with a crippling debt. If the debt was not paid two options remained: they might have to sell their properties, leave their ancestral lands, and move with their families into villages or local towns to look for work.

The second option was that they could have their lands taken over by landlords or 'absentee farmers' who would allow the original peasant family to work the land as *tenant* farmers. The new property owners could keep demanding higher yields of produce from these confiscated lands.

Whatever option occurred was not ultimately the choice of the indebted peasant family. For keeping their lands safe, by trying to work them the best they could, economic powers outside their control had imposed on them an impossible burden. They became victimised for attempting to live an honourable life as peasant farmers.

The parable of the ten pounds would have had a familiar ring to Luke's community members who would have remembered their own victimisation from absentee landlords when landholdings (perhaps in their family for generations) were confiscated or had not been able to produce a satisfactory yield. They would have easily been able to identify with the third servant.

In the time of Jesus and Luke, it was understood that *everything* was limited. In this 'limited good' society the rich only became wealthy at the expense of others becoming poor. In the context of the parable, the act of the third servant, of burying the money without trying to gain extra at the expense of somebody else getting poorer, was the most honourable act. A peasant audience would have praised this servant and regarded the first two as robbers. In the parable, instead of being praised or promoted for doing what was honourable, he is reprimanded by the nobleman.

Luke's audience would not have heard the parable as an encouragement for disciple risk-taking, but as a mirror of life. It would have reminded them that that is how life is: peasant farmers get trampled over, the rich seem to get richer and the poor get poorer or, in the words of the parable, '. . . to all those who have nothing, even what they have will be taken away'. The parable would have mirrored back to Luke's community its recognition that even though God's justice has been inaugurated in the coming of Jesus and injustice will eventually be overthrown, the reign of God is not fully realised. Evil and injustice remain part of the reality with which the disciple has to contend.

The parable would be a sober reminder to some Gospel readers who were thinking that the end was soon, the final coming of Jesus was imminent and that the advantage gained by the wealthy at the expense of the poor would be reversed. The parable reminds Luke's community to settle in for the long haul. Everything anticipated by Jesus' followers in history would happen, but perhaps not so soon.

The introduction to the parable hints at this:

> [Jesus] went on to tell a parable, because he was near Jerusalem, and because they supposed the Kingdom of God was to appear immediately (19:11).

The parable of the ten pounds, read against the cultural background of the first century, would be saying this to Luke's audience: the end is not soon; injustice is still going to be part of the world with which the faithful disciple will have to contend; those who do the honourable thing are not necessarily going to be rewarded for living virtuously. In short, there is still a long way to go before the disciple can rest easy!

This parable, along with the others uttered by Jesus, the Gospel's wisdom teacher and prophet, would have encouraged despondent and searching disciples in Luke's day. The word spoken through this prophet from God would confirm that God was in their midst as powerfully as in the days of Jesus and his first followers. God was active and present despite the difficulties encountered. The urge for justice, as John found when confronted with the injustice experienced by his co-workers at his factory, stems from the action of this same God who moved among Luke's community and was active in the prophetic words and deeds of Jesus.

QUESTIONS

1. What do you understand by 'prophet'? Who do you consider to be prophets today?
2. How is Luke's presentation of Jesus as prophet helpful today in the situations of injustice that we sometimes meet? Can you name some of these situations?
3. Can you identify times when you have taken a prophetic stance? What was the cost for you? How did others help you in taking this stance?

4

Jesus: saviour and healer

Joan had been a teacher all her life. She is married to Tom and they have three children, all of whom married and had sons and daughters. Joan looked forward to her retirement: to the opportunity of pottering around the house and taking up her favourite hobby of watercolour painting with earnestness.

Six months after leaving her teaching career, she went to consult a doctor after complaining of severe neck pain. She was diagnosed with cancer. Joan feels terrified about her future and what will happen to Tom.

Joan's experience opens up the possibility for her to encounter deeply Luke's Jesus. From the earliest chapters of Luke's Gospel, Jesus is presented as the one who has come to liberate human beings from the grip of terror and disaster which assails them. In Jesus, God's compassion for humanity and creation becomes tangible.

In the birth story, Jesus is proclaimed by the angelic messenger as 'God's Son' (1:32,35) and 'Saviour' (2:11). Both these titles portray Jesus as one so close to God that in him the very action that belongs to God, the act of salvation, can also be ascribed to Jesus. Jesus is 'Saviour' whose name in Hebrew means 'Yahweh saves'. In Jesus, God is saving creation and bringing it to wholeness and healing.

The language of 'saviour' and 'salvation' as applied to Jesus occurs in the early and latter parts of the Gospel (1:69, 71,77; 19:9) and continues into the Book of Acts where, in Acts 5:31, Peter exalts Jesus as 'Saviour and Leader'.

Jesus as saviour

This title of *saviour* was a divine name sometimes given to philosophers, physicians, politicans and emperors. Julius

Caesar, for example, was celebrated as the 'revealed god and common *saviour* of human life'. Caesar Augustus was honoured as '*saviour* of the whole world'.

Both Julius Caesar and Caesar Augustus were portrayed like gods and saviours. Both were considered as having the power to deliver human beings from physical, political and moral evil. The high esteem in which these two rulers were held becomes substantially diminished in the light of Luke's presentation of Jesus.

In the Gospel *only Jesus* is called 'saviour'. Luke recognises him as the only one capable of delivering the Gospel's readers from the social and personal evils which afflict them. Jesus is 'saviour' in the fullest sense of the word, with all the political and religious implications associated with this honorific title.

Only through Jesus can people come to a sense of wholeness, of deliverance from social exploitation and of ultimate union with God. There are two ways in which the evangelist spells out this conviction.

Jesus as saviour in the birth story

The first is through the birth story. Luke deliberately situates Jesus' birth against the backdrop of world and political history.

> In those days a decree went out from Emperor Augustus that all the world should be registered. This was the first registration and was taken while Quirinius was governor of Syria. All went to their own towns to be registered (2:1-3).

Luke situates the birth of Jesus against the backdrop of world and political history. Quirinius is governor in Syria and Caesar Augustus issues a decree that all should be registered (2:1). This brings Joseph and Mary to Bethlehem where the true saviour is to be born.

Luke contrasts the self-proclaimed political saviour, Augustus, with the authentic saviour, Jesus. The contrast which Luke creates between Jesus and political leadership continues into the rest of the Gospel.

Jesus as saviour in the miracle stories

The second way in which Luke presents Jesus as saviour and healer to broken human beings is by the miracle stories.

The first scenes of Jesus' public ministry after his pronouncement in the Nazareth synagogue are powerful events of healing and human liberation: he heals the possessed or enfeebled (4:31-41) and those excluded from community life because of disease or paralysis (5:12-26). His saving deeds are restricted neither exclusively to Jews or males, but manifested in Gentiles (7:1-10) and women (7:11-17; 13:10-17).

Underlying Jesus' miraculous activity is his intention that those who have been excluded from community find an authentic welcome. His deeds become a proclamation about God's intention to liberate, heal and bring everyone into divine community. His actions know no boundaries or qualification because no one is to be excluded from God's healing embrace.

This is particularly evident in chapter 8, Luke's most developed presentation of Jesus' saving activity. The four miracle stories in this chapter underscore the liberation brought by Jesus which allows human beings to experience the full power of community.

The storm on the lake

The first story (8:22-25) is set on a lake with Jesus asleep in a storm-lashed boat while his disciples are frightened for their safety. They shout,

> 'Master, Master, we are perishing!' And he woke up and rebuked the wind and the raging waves; they ceased, and there was a calm. He said to them, 'Where is your faith?'(8:24-25).

While the story can be read as a wonderful deed of power by Jesus for his friends, at another level it is a story dealing with community. The storm-tossed boat and its frightened crew could well remind Luke's readers of their own fear in times of apparent disaster, 'apparent' because what can disturb the disciples' faith does not overwhelm Jesus who is relaxed enough to sleep!

The experience of salvation by this frightened community is the experience of 'calm' (8:24) in the midst of the evil that threatens to annihilate it. Jesus is the only one in their midst who can rebuke the raging waves. Only Jesus has the power to liberate the terrified disciples from their deepest fear.

Healing the demoniac

The next miracle story (8:26-39) is the healing of a Gerasene demoniac. The description of the possessed man in the first half of the story shows all the signs of someone entirely cut off from authentic community: he is naked, does not live in a house but in tombs away from the city and shouts at the top of his voice. As a result of Jesus' healing action, the man is 'clothed and in his right mind' (8:35) and, in the final scene, returns to the city to proclaim what Jesus had done for him.

The event is a powerful commentary about the importance which community plays in human healing. Genuine healing occurs when a person is welcomed back into community and participates fully in its life.

For Gospel readers of the Greco-Roman world in the first century, salvation is to be experienced within their own community lives. This insight links to the next two episodes in Luke 8, the resuscitation of a young woman (8:40-42a, 49-56) and the healing of a haemorrhaging older woman (8:42b-48).

The liberation of two women

In both stories Luke draws on Mark's Gospel. The story about the girl who is restored to life surrounds and frames the centrepiece of Luke's literary structure, the healing of a bleeding woman.

Lk 8:40-56

- Story One: Request to heal Jairus' daughter (v40-42a).
- •• Story Two: Healing a haemorrhaging woman (v42b-48).
- Story One (cont): Resuscitation of Jairus' daughter (v49-56).

The two episodes are interconnected. One leads to the other which in turn moves the reader to Jesus' marvellous deed of resuscitation. Both stories emphasise Jesus' power to heal and liberate two people who are regarded as ritually impure.

They have been excluded from the possibility of having union with God because their respective conditions are considered to exclude them from the benefits of community life. Both the young woman who has begun to menstruate and the older woman who is unable to stop menstruating experience genuine healing and 'salvation' through the action of Jesus: they are restored to full community life.

As Luke prepares us for what is to take place, our attention is arrested by the tragedy of the circumstances surrounding the sickness of the daughter of a synagogue official, Jairus; she is Jairus' only child and 'dying' (8:42). She is also twelve years old and therefore of marriageable age.

In the mind of Luke's audience it is clear that the possibilities of a full, fruitful and happy life seem tragically shortened; it looks as though she will die before she can marry, bear children and so allow her prospective husband's household to continue.

Before any resolution can be found to what seems an impossible situation the reader's attention is diverted to a second incident. On Jesus' journey to the official's home,

> . . . there was a woman who had been suffering from haemorrhages for twelve years; and though she had spent all she had on physicians, no one could cure her. She came up behind him and touched the fringe of his clothes, and immediately her haemorrhage stopped. Then Jesus asked, 'Who touched me?' (8:43-45a).

In the world of Luke, blood was a sign of life and death. A bleeding woman was considered to be ritually impure and anything she touched became impure. Jesus would have been regarded as ritually impure, or technically 'unholy' until purified, because a bleeding woman had touched him.

Jesus asks, 'Who touched me?' not because of an impurity ascribed to him by social convention, but because of a healing act of power that had occurred: 'Someone touched me; for I noticed that power had gone out from me' (8:46).

The frightened woman finally comes forward, falls before Jesus and identifies herself as the one immediately healed. Jesus then says to her, 'Daughter, your faith has made you well; go in peace' (8:48). What is translated here as 'made you well' are the Greek words *sesoken se* which literally mean 'has saved you'.

The desperate woman's initiative and spontaneous gesture of touching Jesus' garment, which the reader finally discovers is the result of her faith, brings about an act of physical healing that is ultimately freeing for her. The healing which accompanies Jesus is a salvific action that touches the deepest levels of human existence; it is identified by Luke as 'salvation'.

Luke then returns to the story of Jairus' dying daughter. The reader learns that by now the daughter has died and that Jesus no longer needs to be troubled (8:49). But in words reminiscent of the previous scene Jesus says to the father, 'Do not fear. Only believe, and she will be *saved*' (8:50). Again, healing, salvation and faith are linked.

Jesus goes to the house where the dead woman lies, takes her by the hand and raises her up. The language which Luke uses here for 'raising up' will be used later to describe Jesus' resurrection (cf. 9:22). The connection between what Jesus does to the young woman and what God later does to Jesus in his resurrection is obvious. The resuscitation of Jairus' daughter anticipates the Easter event at the end of the Gospel.

In a concluding deft touch to the story, Jesus hands the young woman to the parents and directs them to give her something to eat. This simple request from Jesus allows Luke to make an essential connection between salvation and the present. The kind of liberation which God offers humanity through the ministry of Jesus, and the kind which Joan deeply seeks as she stares into death's face because of her cancer, does not need to await disclosure in some distant future.

Luke is keen to anchor salvation and healing in the present. The young woman's full restoration to life is symbolised by her being offered something to eat at the initiative of Jesus. For Luke there is a powerful connection between life and food, a point which will be explored in greater detail in the next chapter.

QUESTIONS

1. In Luke, the main form of suffering was people's rejection from community life. From your experience, what are the main forms of suffering that people deal with today?
2. When has someone you know experienced healing, inner strength or a sense of wholeness? What helped to bring this about?
3. How might Luke's presentation of Jesus as saviour and healer be helpful to people struggling today?

5

Jesus: dinner host and guest

Huong arrived in Australia from Vietnam eleven years ago. After a difficult boat voyage and successfully negotiating the stringent immigration procedures of the Australian Government, he made his home in Adelaide with the rest of his family: his mother, father, uncle, grandparents and two brothers and one sister. His home has been broken into twice over the past few months with racist slurs painted across his kitchen wall. Huong wonders why he and his family are subjected to this kind of treatment. A deep sense of rejection looms.

Huong's experience of rejection is not atypical. It is prevalent in our society, but it also provides an unexpected possibility for encountering Luke's Jesus.

A remarkable and consistent portrait that emerges through the Gospel has to do with the way Jesus welcomes those who especially feel rejected and excluded. Nowhere is this more apparent than in the frequency of his meals and the company he keeps at these meals.

This aspect of Jesus' ministry touches into several of the other themes we have already seen: Jesus' meal ministry links to his activity as healer and prophet in word and deed. It also connects to Luke's portrait of Jesus as wisdom source. Just as those searching for Wisdom in the Old Testament come to be fed at her table (Isa 55:1; Sir 51:25; Prov 9: 1-3,5), so too those who desire to know God gather around Jesus to be fed from his table.

As we trace the figure of Jesus throughout the Gospel, in every section he is associated with food, meals and, frequently, controversy which accompanies the kind of meals that he shares.

In the birth story, he is presented as the baby wrapped in bands of cloth and '*lying in the manger*' (2:7,12,16). The reader's initial gaze is directed to a food trough for animals. This is where Jesus is to be found. He is food for creation.

In the opening chapters of his public ministry Jesus scandalises the religious authorities by his carefree attitude to food and fasting. There is something essentially joyous about the feasting Jesus. Luke presents him upsetting those who had expected a more refined, controlled and temperate character. The first explicit criticism about Jesus' meal manners appears in chapter 5 of the Gospel.

Jesus' companions

In this chapter Jesus calls his first disciples (5:1-11) and heals the ritually unclean, a leper (5:12-16) and a paralytic whose sins he forgives. This provokes the ire of the religious authorities who have already determined the way that divine forgiveness should be earned. Finally Jesus calls to discipleship another social deviant, the tax collector* Levi (5:27-28).

The episode which follows (5:29-32) is a festive banquet scene which allows the authorities' fermenting irritation over Jesus' action in the preceding events to be voiced. Their discontent allows Luke to make an important point about Jesus' ministry which will dominate the rest of the Gospel.

> 29Then Levi gave a great banquet for him in his house; and there was a large crowd of tax collectors and others sitting at the table with them. 30The Pharisees and their scribes were complaining to his disciples, saying, 'Why do you eat and drink with tax collectors and sinners?' 31Jesus answered, 'Those who are well have no need of a physician, but those who are sick; 32I have come to call not the righteous but sinners to repentance' (5:29-32).

The kind of companions that Jesus chooses to dine with are those considered to be 'sinners', people regarded as ritually unclean, unholy and excluded from religious practice. In a Mediterranean 'honour-shame'* culture, Jesus would have been judged by the religious leaders as degrading his own honour by feasting with these notorious dinner associates.

Jesus: a 'glutton and drunkard'

There are four fascinating features in this joyful scene. The first concerns the meaning of 'his house' in verse 29. If the house is that of Jesus, then Jesus is the *host* of a banquet prepared for by Levi. Jesus feels free to entertain the socially disreputable.

If we take 'his house' to refer to Levi's house, and this is the most common interpretation, then Jesus is a *guest* of the contemptible. They feel comfortable enough to invite him; he is *like* them; a solidarity exists between them.

As the story progresses and the hostility mounts against Jesus, it becomes clear why he is like those prejudged as despised and unholy. The conventional religious leadership regards Jesus as an irreligious figure who corrupts the sanctity of the community. His prophetic actions in his mealtime behaviour disturb the traditional boundaries of order and purity*. For this reason he is condemned as a religious renegade and heretic, and called 'a glutton and a drunkard, a friend of tax collectors and sinners' (7:34).

The expression 'glutton and drunkard' comes from the Book of Deuteronomy and is used to describe a deceitful and corrupting son who steadfastly refuses to be corrected by his elders. To preserve the integrity of the religious community, the only appropriate judgment on such a person, according to Deuteronomy 21:18f, is death by stoning. In the minds of some, there is a clear link between Jesus and the incorrigible son. Accordingly, Jesus' execution is mandatory.

The scandalous behaviour of Jesus' disciples

A second feature of the meal scene in Luke 5 concerns the addressees of the question, 'Why do *you* eat and drink with tax collectors and sinners?' The question is directed at Jesus' followers about their conduct. They have become implicated in his scandalous behaviour through their association with him.

In Mark's Gospel the question is framed differently, 'Why does *he* eat with tax collectors and sinners?' (Mk 2:16). In Mark's Gospel Jesus' conduct is under scrutiny.

By the time Luke writes, the subject of the question has been expanded to include all those who follow Jesus. In other words, the prophetic attitude of Jesus reflected in his meal ministry is now a publicly identifiable characteristic of the community of disciples that gathers around him.

It could well be for Luke's readers that their welcome and communion with social deviants at their eucharistic table is being condemned by civil and religious authorities as scandalous and socially destructive.

Jesus' meals: occasions of liberation

A third point emerges from verse 31. It is Jesus who responds to the questioners. He speaks on behalf of the disciples. Their notorious conduct in festive celebration has the authorisation of Jesus himself. His response takes the form of a wisdom saying which accentuates the essentially healing dimension of his ministry: 'Those who are well have no need of a physician, but those who are sick'.

This echoes the statement Jesus issued at the beginning of his public ministry in the synagogue at Nazareth (Luke 4) which foreshadowed the program of his ministry of healing: he had come to bring release to those who experienced imprisonment.

His meal ministry was a visible expression of this liberation. His meals were essentially powerful parables of God's abundant liberating joy over the whole of creation, including those who had felt excluded from divine communion by a legalistic religious leadership.

Finally, verse 32 offers a further summary statement of the purpose of Jesus' ministry. He reminds his antagonists and all those in Luke's community who would like to restrict God's graciousness that he has 'come to call not the righteous but sinners to repentance'.

The word which Jesus speaks and acts in his mealtime conduct is intended for those who are 'sinners', people whose conduct excludes them from the main stream of life.

For Luke's Jesus, only those who are open and recognise that they cannot control God or claim themselves holy by their use of power, politics or wealth are called to discipleship. They are called to 'repentance', to a change of life that sees reality in a new and unexpected way. Through Jesus they are invited to recognise that all who are open to God's action, and especially publicly declared 'sinners', are prime candidates for union with God.

Jesus: source of delight and merry-making

Jesus' coming is an occasion of delight and merry-making. For this reason the next scene has Jesus excoriating his adversaries (5:33-39). They have condemned his disciples who do not fast like those of John the Baptist or the authorities, but 'eat and drink' (5:33). Jesus reminds his opponents, 'You cannot make wedding guests fast while the bridegroom is with them, can you?' (5:34). Jesus' presence brings people to celebrate life. Through him God rejoices in the world. The presence of Jesus needs to be celebrated not lamented; feasting rather than fasting is appropriate; in fact encouraged.

These aspects celebrated in this meal scene in Luke 5 continue in the Gospel. Luke dots the remaining chapters with mention of food, meal scenes and miracle stories of feeding hungry people. Banquets provide the opportunity for discipleship-teaching about the reign of God.

Chapter 14 is especially pertinent. The chapter is a meal scene which becomes, in the tradition of the classic Greco-Roman banquet, an occasion for Luke to present Jesus like a Greek philosopher imparting wisdom and social truths to his reclining pupils. The teaching that Jesus gives in this meal setting overturns the conventional 'wisdom' upheld by his antagonists. The opening verse of the chapter sets the scene for a potentially explosive situation ignited by Jesus' teaching.

> On one occasion when Jesus was going to a house of the leader of the Pharisees to eat a meal on the sabbath, they were watching him closely. . . (14:1).

The meal and the accompanying teaching which unfolds in the rest of the chapter occur in the house of a religious official. The unspecified 'they' in the verse refers to the religious leaders. This helps to heighten the tension in the scene as the feasting Jesus has his conduct scrutinised by his critics.

Jesus teaches his audience about the true purpose of the Sabbath (14:1-6), honour in selecting one's position at the table (14:7-11), the most suitable guests to invite to dinner (14:12-14), and a concluding powerful parable which reveals the most appropriate and divinely sought after candidates for the heavenly banquet (14:15-24).

Jesus at a Meal (14:1-24)

Teaching 1: About Sabbath (v 1-6)
Teaching 2: About honour at table (v 7-11)
Teaching 3: About dinner guests (v 12-14)
Teaching 4: Parable – candidates for the heavenly banquet (v 15-24)

Traditional dining protocol allowed meals to become a means by which a 'patron' (the host and usually a male) could show his largesse to his 'clients' (the meal guests). Guests would in turn be expected to reciprocate the meal favour by inviting the host to a banquet. This was an established cultural mechanism that enabled the patron's honour to be increased in the eyes of others.

This system of reciprocal generosity could be undertaken only by guests who had the means to reciprocate. Meals were therefore shared between people of the same social status. Only they could show the host the appropriate honour his status demanded and reinforce their relationship as client-guests to the patron-host.

People without means, social misfits or the physically impaired were naturally excluded from meals to which society's elite* were invited. Someone from the elite who shared a meal with others from the lower end of the social spectrum would risk incurring the shame of family and being cut out of the social network of the privileged class.

Jesus' teaching completely subverts this system of customary propriety:

> 'When you give a luncheon or dinner, do not invite your friends or your brothers or your relatives or rich neighbours, in case they may invite you in return, and you would be repaid. But when you give a banquet, invite the poor, the crippled, the lame and the blind. And you will be blessed, because they cannot repay you, for you will be repaid at the resurrection of the righteous' (14:12-14).

The guests at Jesus' proposed banqueting scene are those who are socially excluded. All are to be invited. As the next parable of the great dinner makes clear (14:15-24), the 'poor, the crippled, the blind, and the lame' are able to accept the invitation to a meal intended for all. The parable reflects the inclusivity of the eschatological meal prepared by God.

Jesus' meal teaching in chapter 14 reinforces the kinds of eucharistic gatherings typical in Luke's community: festive meals that do not keep a strict code of reciprocity common in the Greco-Roman world. They are celebrations which are weighted in favour of the socially-ostracised and reflect a largesse which is of God. These meals go against the cultural trend of meals shared with people of the same social rank; they transgress social and cultural barriers.

There is one last scene towards the end of the Gospel which deserves special comment. It is an event which would not be ordinarily associated with Jesus' meal ministry, the account of Jesus' death (23:39-43).

The dying Jesus promises to the thief who repents, 'Truly I tell you, today you will be with me in Paradise' (23:43). This promise of Paradise was a promise of bequeathed salvation which Isaiah associated with the choicest wines and richest foods (Isa 25:6-9). The faithful Israelite would be able to experience the most delicious banquet with God. It is this kind of banqueting experience which Jesus promises the condemned criminal.

Summary

Luke's emphasis on food and feasting comes out of a very profound appreciation in the Greco-Roman world of the symbolic value placed on meals. To eat with another was more than simply a way of fulfilling a basic need to satisfy one's hunger; a shared meal was a sign of a deeper solidarity which existed between dining companions. Through the meal, life projects became intertwined with each other, the household as the primary unit within Greco-Roman society was established, family kinship ties were strengthened and community identity confirmed.

All these insights are contained in Jesus' meal activity and offer a way of summarising Luke's presentation of Jesus as meal host and guest: Jesus eats with those who, like Huong and his family, feel alien or like foreigners. Jesus' action reflects the action of a God who is essentially hospitable.

But there is something more which Luke wants to emphasise: Jesus' festive meals are enacted parables of God's *delight* about the whole of creation. Through Jesus' prophetic action, God seeks to celebrate human beings. No one is to be excluded from this celebration of divine ecstasy.

QUESTIONS

1. Can you recall any situation in which people felt excluded, considered unworthy or unsatisfactory? What are the reasons for this exclusion?
2. What are your own experiences of meals? With whom do you find yourself eating? When was the last time you really *enjoyed* a meal? What were the circumstances?
3. When do people seem to really celebrate? How is celebrating and merry-making experienced in local church communities?
4. What helps others to come to a sense of a joyful, festive God? What contribution would Luke's presentation of Jesus as dinner host and guest make to this?

6

Jesus: innocent martyr

Cassandra is the beautiful three-year-old daughter of Jim and Anne. She is their only child. Cassandra's unusual convulsions late one night forced her parents to take her to hospital. Medical tests suggested a brain disorder which began to affect her respiration. Looking down at their tiny daughter hooked up to a respirator Jim and Anne wonder what her future might be.

As she lies in this hospital bed, they imagine what it must be for parents in other parts of the world to keep vigil beside their sick or dying child. They are shattered by what has happened. They wonder about God's presence and what God might be saying to them through this pain. Deep within themselves a conflict rages between what they have heard preached about a loving God and their own experience of the critical sickness of their only child.

Conflict is not foreign to us. It occurs in moments of struggle, especially at times when we feel helpless as we see someone innocent suffer. At these times we seek to see how God can act within the trauma of such a situation. Luke's community members also knew conflict and struggle as they sought to understand God's purpose in their lives.

One of Luke's narrative techniques for allowing the Gospel's story to unfold is through the conflict that develops in the interaction between Jesus and the religious and political authorities. This conflict is alluded to in the opening chapters of the Gospel (Lk 1-3), unfolds in Jesus' public ministry (Lk 4-8), is accentuated in the narrative of the journey to Jerusalem (Lk 9-19) and reaches its climax in the circumstances surrounding Jesus' passion, death and resurrection (Lk 20-24). The conflict is essentially between the plan of God revealed in Jesus and the plan ascribed to God by the religious hierarchy.

Mary's song: reversal of fortune

In the opening chapter the song placed on the lips of Mary praises the way God has acted and shown compassion throughout history (1:46-56). God's action has brought about a reversal of fortune and expectation; the proud have been scattered, the powerful brought down and the rich sent away empty, while the lowly have been lifted up and the hungry filled.

This reversal of fortune brought about by God becomes the basis for the conflict which will occur between Jesus and his enemies. Jesus represents the divine action and plan of God. His opponents present a different plan. The image of God presented in Mary's song of praise is continued through Jesus.

Towards the end of the infancy narrative there are two scenes which remind the reader of the discord which will accompany Jesus' future ministry. The first is the scene of his circumcision (2:22-38).

Jesus in the temple

Mary and Joseph bring Jesus to the temple to consecrate him to God as prescribed by the Mosaic Law (in Exodus 13:1-2). This action in the temple occurs deliberately right at the centre of Jewish political, economic and religious life. To this same centre Jesus will return for the finale of his public ministry.

As Jesus' parents bring him to the temple they also meet the spirit-inspired Simeon who had been 'looking forward to the consolation of Israel' (2:25). Simeon highlights two aspects of Jesus' future ministry: (1) through him God's light will be shed upon all peoples; (2) Jesus will also be a source of division and conflict which will affect even his own family. As Simeon says to Mary,

> 'This child is destined for the falling and the rising of many in Israel, and to be a sign that will be opposed so that the inner thoughts of many will be revealed – and a sword will pierce your own soul too' (2:34-35).

Simeon prepares the reader for the opposition and rejection that will be experienced by Jesus and those faithful to him (including Mary). In this earliest chapter Simeon announces the suffering which will accompany Jesus and prepares the reader for Jesus' death in the Gospel's final chapters.

The second scene is the final one in the infancy story in which Jesus is found in the temple sitting among its teachers and questioning them (2:41-52). His questions could indicate that he is seeking to learn and grow in wisdom. Certainly this is confirmed by the context which frames this scene in which Jesus' growth in wisdom is noted (2:40,52).

However, Luke presents the infant Jesus in a *sitting* position *among* the official temple teachers, in the posture of a teacher, questioning the other teachers. This might suggest something else. Perhaps in this we have a development of the opposition prophesied by Simeon. Luke is presenting this young person now in his 'Father's house' (2:49) as an alternative teacher who can authoritatively question the orthodox teachers of Judaism.

If this is the case, then as the Gospel moves towards Jesus' public ministry, the forces of opposition are already intensifying. Confrontation and dispute seem inevitable.

Jesus in conflict with the authorities

The reader does not have to go too much further before the opposition predicted in the infancy story becomes explicit: in his preaching in his hometown synagogue at Nazareth, Jesus raises the ire of his listeners (4:16-30). They interpret his message about a God who is concerned for all, not just the Israelite people, as provocative and heretical. They hustle him out of the town, to the brow of the hill on which Nazareth sits, intending to throw him to his death. In his first public act of preaching, Jesus finds himself in serious conflict even with his own neighbours.

Through chapters 5 to 6 there is a cycle of five stories in which Jesus clashes with the religious establishment. Each conflict is about Jesus' authority, his ability to interpret the Mosaic Law authentically, especially in its application of the purity regulations which seek to define the truly blessed of God. Jesus reinterprets a conservative application of these laws. His ministry to the unholy and despised pushes out the social boundaries which define God's holy people.

In 6:6-11 Jesus publicly heals someone in a synagogue on the Sabbath, in a religious place on the sacred day of the week. By his defiant action and words ('I ask you, is it lawful to do good or to do harm on the Sabbath, to save life or to destroy it?'), Jesus challenges the official legal interpretation of the meaning of Sabbath. His celebration of the Sabbath as a day of liberation and healing intended by God contradicts the more restrictive view upheld by some religious authorities. Luke's final comment in verse 11 sets the tone for what will eventuate in the final chapters:

> But [the religious leaders] were filled with fury and discussed with one another what they might do to Jesus (6:11).

This scheming attitude of the authorities remains in the background of Jesus' ministry in Galilee and journey to Jerusalem and is evident in his conversations with them in 7:36; 11:37; 14:1. Not until Jesus' final triumphant entry into Jerusalem does their hostile attitude develop into murderous threats.

> Every day Jesus was teaching in the temple. The chief priests, the scribes, and the leaders of the people kept looking for a way to kill him... (19:47-48).

This comment occurs after Jesus weeps over Jerusalem (19:41-44) and enters the temple, cleansing it of its sellers and reclaiming it for God (19:45-47). In the final chapters the controversy from the leaders over Jesus' authority returns. Here the conflict has reached fever pitch and the religious officials look for a way to kill him:

> Now the festival of Unleavened Bread, which is called the Passover, was near. The chief priests and the scribes were looking for a way to put Jesus to death... (22:1-2).

The 'conflict' motif

Why is Luke interested in the conflict between Jesus and the religious officials? The conflict motif in the Gospel is important for three reasons.

First, conflict becomes a literary thread or device which engages the readers' interest in the plot and its unfolding. This device is announced in the infancy story, is explicit in the early and latter chapters of the Gospel and remains present as a narrative backdrop in the intervening chapters.

Second, as already noted, the conflict motif allows Luke to highlight an important theological point. The controversy which Jesus experiences reveals the radical presentation of God revealed in his ministry that rivals the image of God predetermined by the Jewish religious and political leaders. Jesus presents a God who is hospitable to society's outcasts. They are God's people. Israel's leaders would prefer a more restrictive view of who constitutes God's chosen.

Jesus: faithful witness

Third, the conflict theme allows Luke to add another dimension to the portrait of Jesus. Luke presents Jesus as God's faithful witness. Throughout his public career, Jesus faithfully witnesses to God's justice and compassion for all people. In the passion he is unflinching in his witness to God's plan. He does not deviate from the final journey he must undergo despite the opposition mounted against him.

In the Gospel and Acts, Jesus is never explicitly or directly called God's 'witness'. Witnessing is rather the act accredited to Jesus' disciples. They witness to Jesus' deeds and words in the Gospel (21:13) and through the suffering they endure at the hands of the civil and religious authorities in the Book of Acts (4:33; 14:3; 15:8; 23:11; 26:22).

However, throughout the Gospel it is clear that Jesus is God's witness. This comes to light in the passion story. Here there is an important scene in which Jesus is unwittingly and ironically identified as the only true and authentic witness.

In the morning after his arrest, Jesus is before the Council of the Jewish leaders who seek to incriminate him as a self-deluded heretic presuming divine authority. They seek to know his identity. Jesus refuses to respond directly to their description of him as the Messiah: 'If you are not the Messiah, tell us' (22:67). Instead, he chooses to speak of himself on his own terms,

> [69]'But from now on the Human One will be seated on the right hand of the power of God.' [70]All asked, 'Are you, therefore, the Son of God?' He said to them, 'You yourselves say that I am'. [71]They said, What further *witness* do we need? For we have heard it ourselves from his own mouth!' (22:69-71. *Author's translation*).

Jesus accepts the Council's own description of him as the Son of God ('You yourselves say that I am'). They ironically confirm him as the one who can reveal God's identity because of his closeness to God. For this reason they say, 'What further *witness* do we need?' Unwittingly, they have identified Jesus as the ultimate witness. There is no further need of witnesses because Jesus has, throughout the Gospel, unequivocally witnessed to himself, his relationship with God and the kind of God revealed in his ministry. This witness to God continues to the cross.

Jesus: innocent martyr

The Greek word translated as 'witness' in verse 71 is *marturias* from which is derived the English word 'martyr'. Jesus is Luke's definitive martyr who witnesses to God's justice and care for humanity. It is because of his steadfast fidelity to God that Jesus finds himself in conflict with the political and religious hierarchy who regard him as a heretic more concerned with welcoming social pariahs than with the observance of the Mosaic tradition as interpreted by official legal commentators. Jesus' preaching, healing and meal ministry reveal a different understanding and appreciation of the ways of God.

As we have seen, in the closing chapters of the Gospel the conflict between Jesus and the Jerusalem leadership heightens with its final resolution in Jesus' death. Moreover, this resolution occurs as Jesus is explicitly and unmistakably presented as a martyr. This presentation is accompanied with the constant echo of his innocence voiced by the most unlikely characters.

In his trial Jesus is declared innocent by Pilate three times: first, before the Jewish religious leaders Pilate attests that he finds 'no basis for an accusation against [Jesus]' (23:4); then, after Jesus is returned from Herod's scrutiny Pilate again affirms that Jesus is not guilty of the charges laid against him (23:14); finally, Pilate adds Herod's name to a definitive declaration of Jesus' innocence:

> 'I have examined him in your presence and have not found this man guilty of any of your charges against him. Neither has Herod, for he sent him back to us. Indeed, he has done nothing to deserve death...' (23:14-16).

To this attestation of Jesus' innocence is added that of a convicted criminal. The words the criminal utters to his crucified accomplice unmistakably exonerate Jesus.

> 'Do you not fear God, since you are under the same sentence of condemnation? And we indeed have been condemned justly, for we are getting what we deserve for our deeds, but this man has done nothing wrong...' (23:40-41).

The criminal's proclamation of Jesus' guiltlessness is finally confirmed by a Roman centurion, the last of the passion narrative's gallery of unusual characters marshalled by Luke confirming Jesus in his innocence.

> When the centurion saw what had taken place, he praised God and said, 'Certainly this man was innocent' (23:47).

The witness of the criminal and the centurion frame the Gospel's climactic death scene in which Jesus dies promising paradise to the repentant, and entrusting himself to his God.

Luke's point seems clear: here in the death of Jesus is God's revelation of the innocent One whose life of faithful witness culminates in this moment of death, in the ultimate act of martyrdom which is the continuity and summation of a life lived faithfully.

The revelation of a restrictive interpretation of the Torah, which Jesus had been contesting throughout the Gospel, is now perceived and pronounced by two most unlikely characters considered excluded from God's reign: a criminal and a Gentile military leader. Their pronouncement confirms a central truth which Luke has been keen to underscore throughout the Gospel, that God's compassion and revelation found in Jesus is available to the whole of humanity.

Jesus: righteous one

What is translated as 'innocent' in the centurion's pronouncement of verse 47 is the Greek word *dikaios*. This literally means 'righteous', a word sometimes misunderstood in English. The final human declaration which comes on the death of Jesus publicly proclaims that he is one with God. Jesus is faithful, virtuous and guiltless who has acted rightly and justly throughout his life.

It is important to note that Jesus never declares himself as 'righteous'. Such 'self-righteousness' is a person's *own* declaration of worthiness and moral rectitude. This is attributed by Jesus' enemies to their own conduct. They consider themselves the only authentic interpreters of the mind of God as expressed in the Mosaic Law or Torah. Throughout the Gospel it is the 'righteousness' of Jesus, God's opinion of Jesus' ministry finally articulated by the centurion, which is in conflict with the 'self-righteousness' of the religious establishment.

The conviction of Jesus' innocence articulated by an extraordinarily varied group of fallible human characters in the passion narrative prepares the reader for God's own ultimate declaration of Jesus. This is revealed in the events of Easter day with Jesus' resurrection and ascension (24:1-12, 50-53). These divine actions vindicate Jesus as the innocent and just one who continues to witness to God even at the point of death. Like the Jewish martyrs before him and those who would experience undeserved suffering after him, Jesus is the innocent martyr *par excellence*. To disciples throughout history, like Anne and Jim at the bedside of their critically ill daughter, seeking to witness to God despite unwarranted persecution and unjust suffering, Luke directs their gaze to the innocent, suffering Jesus.

QUESTIONS

1. Conflict is a theme that Luke uses in the Gospel. What are the kinds of conflict that you have experienced in your life? What are their causes?
2. In what situations does another's suffering seem particularly unjust or undeserved? What is your reaction to these experiences?
3. In these experiences of unjust or innocent suffering, how does God seem? What is the sense of God which dominates?
4. When do people find themselves speaking or turning to God? How would Luke's presentation of Jesus as innocent martyr be helpful?
5. Whom would you consider contemporary martyrs? From what countries do such recent martyrs come?

7

Jesus: the human one

Jeff has been drinking since the age of twelve. As a young lad and after school he would often join a couple of his friends for a drinking session with alcohol stolen from the neighbourhood liquor store. As he grew older, the drinking became more serious. Parties turned into all night sessions. Friends were determined by how much liquor they could offer. Enjoyment was measured by quantity of liquor consumed.

In recent moments of sobriety, Jeff recognises that he has a problem. He feels ashamed and guilt-ridden. He looks back over the years and recognises the pattern. Everything seems difficult. His life appears so complex he does not know what to do or how to get himself out of this mess. He is searching for insight into his own situation.

To people like Jeff seeking to deal with the anguish of their lives, Luke presents Jesus as one who can most deeply identify with people in their struggles. For Luke, Jesus is the pre-eminent figure and principal character in the Gospel story. He is central to Luke's community and pivotal for all who feel afflicted in any way.

The centrality of Jesus to Luke's struggling community is suggested by the multiplicity of images that Luke associates with him. Some of these we have already reflected on. It is also suggested by the variety of titles applied to him. Jesus is called:

Messiah or *Christ* (2:11,26; 3:15; 4:41; 9:20; 20:41; 22:67, etc.),
Lord (4:8,12; 7:13,19; 10:1,39,41),
saviour (3:11; 4:42; 13:32),
Son of God (1:32,35; 4:3,9, 41; 8:28; 22:70),
servant (7:7; Acts 3:13,36; 4:27,30),
Son of David (18:38,39); 20:41,44),

holy one (1:35; 4:34),
leader (Acts 5:31),
righteous one (1:17; 23:47,50),
teacher (7:40; 9:38, 10:25; 11:45, etc.)
Son of man (5:24; 6:5; 12:10, 19:10, ff.).

All of these titles seek to express something of the uniqueness of Jesus, his absolute closeness to God and his deep compassion for and solidarity with human beings. In a latter theological development at the Council of Chalcedon in 451, this uniqueness will be expressed in terms of Jesus being declared as truly divine and truly human. The foundations for this theological statement are laid in the late first century by the Gospel writers, including Luke.

Jesus' intimacy with God

Jesus' intimacy with God is emphasised from the beginning of the Gospel. Luke unequivocally presents Jesus as *from* God and God's agent. This is obvious in several ways:

His conception is announced by a divine messenger who indicates the divine origin of Jesus (1:34-35); he acts under the agency of God's Spirit to seek baptism and experience temptation (3:21-22; 4:1-13); he declares himself as anointed by God's very Spirit (4:18); he announces his liberating ministry in the Nazareth synagogue because of God's spirit upon him (4:19); his unique relationship with God is frequently described by Luke; he consults God frequently in prayer, discerning his ministry at significant moments (3:21; 6:12; 9:31; 24:46); by God's action he is raised from the dead, a real event emphasised especially in the Risen Jesus' eating broiled fish before his disciples' eyes (24:41-42); finally, Jesus ascends to be exalted by God (24:50-51).

All these scenes and events remind Luke's readers that Jesus is close to God. He is from God and acts in God' name.

The final scene of the ascension reflects this particularly (24:50-53). This scene brings to completion Jesus' passion, death and resurrection, rounds off the Gospel and prepares for the Acts of the Apostles.

> . . . he led them out as far as Bethany, and, lifting up his hands, he blessed them. While he was blessing them, he withdrew from them and was carried up into heaven. And they worshipped him, and returned to Jerusalem with great joy; and they were continually in the temple blessing God (24:50-53).

Luke's language is deliberately liturgical. Jesus is presented as the High Priest bestowing God's blessing on those assembled. This completes the blessing which Zechariah was unable to give at the beginning of the Gospel (1:21-23). Through the scene's spatial language of Jesus' departure, with him being 'carried up to heaven', the reader is left with a sense of completeness.

Now Jesus' ministry, begun among his community of disciples, will be continued afresh as High Priest interceding before God on behalf of his disciples throughout history. He is worshipped like God and the disciples return to the temple with joy, a theme evident from the Gospel's earliest chapters, praising the God of Jesus. The Gospel concludes where it began, in the temple.

Jesus' solidarity with human beings

The intimate connection between God and Jesus which Luke paints throughout the Gospel is balanced by images and titles of Jesus that express his compassion and solidarity with human beings. Peter's Pentecost sermon in Acts 2 addressed to the Jerusalem crowd uses specifically human language in speaking of Jesus.

> 'You are the Israelites, listen to what I have to say: *Jesus of Nazareth*, a *man* attested to you by God with deeds of power, wonders, and signs that God did through him among you . . .' (Acts 2:22-23).

Peter's speech almost seems like an early Christian creed. The description of Jesus emphasises his human origins; he is 'of Nazareth', an identifiable small village in the hill country of Galilee. This also suggests a family and kinship structure, the basis of village life in a peasant rural economy. Jesus is also called 'a man', a human being with a specific sexual identity.

Through his human identity and association with a geographically located village, Jesus becomes the agent of God. This agency, according to Luke, is essentially linked to the human features that circumscribe the Jewish Jesus who is 'among you'. From what Peter says, the agency is also revealed through his 'deeds of power, wonders, and signs', tangible or visible expression of God's activity in Jesus.

In summary, Luke's creedal statement about Jesus in Acts from the lips of Peter, brings together the two essential perspectives from which Luke's readers are invited to view Jesus, his relationship to God and his rootedness in the Jewish world connecting him to all human beings.

Nowhere is Jesus' intimate bonding with God and humanity better presented than in Luke's genealogy of Jesus (3:23-38) strategically located between his baptism (3:21-22) and temptation (4:1-13). All three passages deal with Jesus' identity, his closeness to God (through his baptism), his solidarity with humanity (in his temptations) and his connection with the Israelite people and their history (expressed by the genealogy).

The genealogy begins with his immediate ancestry and concludes by naming Jesus as 'son of Adam, son of God' (3:38). These are Jesus' original forebears: *God* and *Adam*. Jesus is *God's Son* and also *Adam's Son*. The genealogy highlights the link between the two. Jesus cannot be the 'son' of one without being, at the same time, the 'son' of the other.

The name 'Adam' is derived from the Hebrew word *adamah*, meaning 'person of the earth'. Luke's genealogy explicitly connects Jesus with the first human being created by God from the soil (Gen 2:7). This 'earthy' bond which Jesus has with humanity is expressed in one other way in the Gospel, through Luke's use of the title 'Son of Man', more appropriately translated as 'the human one'.

Jesus: the human one

Luke frequently places this title, 'the human one', on the lips of Jesus. The title is found throughout the Gospel, frequently expressing Jesus' human condition and sometimes associated with his imminent suffering (for example, 5:24; 6:5; 9:22,24; 12:10; 19:10; 22:22,48). In the context of Jesus' passion and death, the title takes on even greater significance.

In the events leading up to his arrest Jesus twice calls himself 'the human one', each occasion refers to his betrayal; the first at the farewell meal (22:22), the second as Judas prepared to betray him with a kiss:

> 'Judas, is it with a kiss that you betray the *human one*?' (22:48. *Author's translation*).

At these two most critical moments when the forces of evil are arraigned against him and Jesus turns to his companions for support, he recognises that it is by the very deed of one of his own that the drama of his passion and death will unfold. Here, Jesus is never more vulnerable. He enters into the events of his passion as an innocent victim of another's weakness and compromise. Jesus in his vulnerability is in solidarity with all those who have been betrayed.

This final section of the Gospel presents the human Jesus at another level. In his betrayal and throughout his passion he is presented as God's chosen one who represents all humanity; during his trial he is adamantly uncompromising in his response to his accusers; at the moment of death his concern is for others while his attention is riveted on God; he dies forgiving those who execute him and refusing to test God by seeking self-salvation.

In the final chapter of the Gospel, as the early morning light breaks and the perplexed women discover Jesus' tomb empty, 'two men', divine messengers, explain the reason for the tomb's emptiness. They remind the women about Jesus' self-description as the 'human one' destined to die and rise. This remembrance recalls during his public ministry in Galilee Jesus' own assessment of his death, the penultimate deed in his ministry:

> 'Why do you seek the living among the dead? He is not here, but has been raised. Remember how he said to you, while still in Galilee, that the *human one* must be handed over to sinners, and be crucified and on the third day rise' (24:5-7. *Author's translation*).

The women, and Luke's audience, are reminded of what Jesus told them while ministering in Galilee. While journeying towards Jerusalem Jesus prepares his disciples for the final events that await him.

He calls himself 'the human one' because what he will experience in his death and resurrection encapsulates that which awaits every human being faithful to God. What happens to Jesus is divinely ordained; it 'must' happen. This is not to say that Luke envisages a vindictive or punishing God who inevitably controls Jesus' destiny to the point that he must limply succumb to the suffering which God has prepared for him. Rather, the expression 'must' suggests that what Luke's Jesus experiences is interpreted by him *only* against the backdrop of God's divine plan of salvation for human beings.

In other words, what Luke is saying through Jesus is that the total experience of human fragility, expressed most fully in death, can be integrated with God. Suffering, death and God's compassionate care of human beings are not mutually exclusive.

Luke's Easter message about Jesus

This interpretation of human existence and destiny does not allow death the final word. There is a life initiated by God which awaits every human being beyond the grave. For this reason, the Easter proclamation becomes central: 'He has been raised' (a more accurate translation of the Greek than 'He has risen') proclaims that what is done to Jesus is God's act. God is the initiator of the act which causes Jesus to rise from death and vindicates the faithful ministry of this innocent sufferer and 'righteous' one.

This Easter message which the women are invited to remember and about which they will witness to the male disciples in the next scene (24:9-12), sums up the whole of Jesus' ministry. It becomes the keystone upon which the disciples' faith in the God of Jesus is built.

It is here, at this climax in his life, that Jesus is presented as 'the human one', God's beloved one who foreshadows the destiny of every faithful human being open to the God revealed through Jesus. He is presented as God's anointed one who shows to Luke's readers how to live as authentic human beings. His ministry offers hope to a struggling people. His cause for justice, at the cost of his own safety and life, offers hope to a struggling community.

Jesus is Luke's trustworthy paradigm for Jeff struggling with his alcoholism and for all who seek liberation and hope in their world. As the Gospel's 'human one' he is able to identify with those who are struggling, marginalised and ostracised.

QUESTIONS

1. When have you felt God close to you?
2. When have you felt God's distance or absence?
3. In what situations in our world would you like God to be involved?
4. What experiences do people consider are the 'most human'? What implication would this have on the way we look at Luke's presentation of Jesus as 'the human one'?

8

Jesus in Luke's Gospel: a summary

Throughout the Gospel Luke continually directs the reader's gaze to Jesus. As the Gospel's principal protagonist, he is the one in whom God's plan for salvation is revealed and the only one through whom people can experience what it means to be truly liberated.

Jesus' words and deeds

Jesus proclaims this liberation through his ministry of word and deed. His words speak to the real needs of people. They address those who feel broken and separated from full participation in community. His words confront the injustices and structures of a religious and political establishment which tend to keep the majority of people disempowered.

Jesus' deeds confirm what he says; he seeks out the lost, hurting, sick, poor and rejected and invites them into a new community of equals. The egalitarian structure of this community of disciples represents alternative economic and political possibilities for a renewed Israel. These in turn bring into conflict the socio-political and economic structures reinforced by the religious hierarchy.

The sub-theme of conflict between Jesus and the religious officials which runs through Luke's Gospel mirrors the political reality experienced in Luke's own community. This conflict highlights the problems of the political and economic value system which is perpetuated by civil leaders.

Part of Luke's agenda is to help later disciples of Jesus negotiate a political system, which discriminates against the poor and vulnerable in favour of the powerful and wealthy.

Luke's Jesus of Greco-Roman culture

The portrait of Jesus in Luke's Gospel is designed for subsequent generations of disciples. It is intended to insert them fully into the Greco-Roman culture of the late first century Mediterranean world. He is a gregarious and cosmopolitan Jesus who moves between the various social classes found in any Greco-Roman urban setting. He is presented from the outset as one who can take on the Roman imperial system. He is like, but superior to, an Augustus whose reign brings true peace. A philosopher who refuses to be trapped by the technical arguments of his antagonists. A healer to whom the sick and handicapped come. Luke's Jesus has a divine authority which enables him to interpret the Torah. His freedom to mix with the socially disreputable confounds Jerusalem's officialdom.

Luke's Jesus is a colourful, dynamic, scandalous and compassionate figure whose style of life and ministry is presented as a model or paradigm for the ongoing life of the Christian community.

This is even more evident in Luke's second volume, the Acts of the Apostles, when the one who proclaimed God's reign to liberate human beings becomes, in turn, the one proclaimed by the Christian community. Jesus is central to both volumes.

A cursory glance at the Book of Acts shows the prominence which the preached Jesus assumes in the community of disciples, first in Jerusalem, then in Judea, Samaria and throughout the rest of the Mediterranean world culminating in Rome. The last words in Acts focus on Paul's preaching ministry in Rome and summarise this homiletic development. While Paul's preaching concerns the reign of God it also concentrates on Jesus:

> And [Paul] lived there two whole years at his own expense, and welcomed all who came to him, preaching the kingdom of God and teaching about the Lord Jesus Christ quite openly and unhindered (Acts 28:30-31).

These two preoccupations of the preaching of the first Christians and reflected in this concluding scene in Acts, its stress on God's reign and the ministry of Jesus, are intimately linked. For Luke and subsequent Christians, the active presence of God in their lives is tangibly evident in Jesus and the ministry continued by the Christian community. As the readers in Luke's day are reminded through Peter's address to the elders and rulers in Jerusalem,

> 'There is salvation in no one else, for there is no other name under heaven given among mortals by which we must be saved' (Acts 4:12).

Luke presents Jesus as pivotal for the life of the Christian community; he is the agent of God's liberation of human beings ('salvation'); he is the climax of God's action through history as expressed in the story of Israel; he is also at the veey heart of human history.

Summary and review

Four implications emerge from this brief study of Luke's presentation of Jesus.

1. The Gospel and the Acts of the Apostles represent Luke's passion to communicate anew to a later generation of disciples. These followers of Jesus are chronologically and geographically removed from the historical Jesus and the first group of disciples. Luke seeks to ground this new audience in the origins of their faith; the foundation of this faith is Jesus. The need will always remain for the Chris-

tian community constantly to return to Jesus as the focus of its faith in seeking to discover the relevance of the message of Jesus.

2. The evangelist employs a variety of images and titles to communicate the ongoing significance of Jesus for the community of disciples in history. This variety of images, which includes portraits of Jesus as wisdom figure, prophet, saviour and healer, dinner host and guest, innocent martyr and 'human one', suggests that for the evangelist no *one* image can ever communicate adequately or exhaust the relevance of Jesus. Luke's practice suggests the legitimacy of exploring other images for Jesus which could be more culturally relevant expressions to contemporary Christians. How Luke comes to this variety of images moves us to the next point.

3. In assisting the Gospel's readers to focus on Jesus, the evangelist draws on the traditional images received from the written and oral sources referred to in the opening verses of the Gospel (1:1-4). The evangelist also sees the need to nuance and supplement these images in a way which makes the Gospel story more suited for a predominantly Greco-Roman, Gentile audience.

Luke, for example, borrows from traditional images and titles about Jesus that come from Mark's Gospel. The images of Jesus as dinner host and guest, prophet and the 'human one', are a few that Luke inherits from Mark. These are nuanced to make their relevance more obvious for a group of Christians living in a different part of the Mediterranean world some fifteen years later.

Luke also employs images which are unique to the third Gospel. These are suggested from the cultural context of the audience. The presentation of Jesus as 'saviour', for example, is partly borrowed from the philosophical, legal and political world of Luke's readers. No qualification or apology is given for the transference of this title to Jesus. This again suggests that anything can be used legitimately to explore the relevance of Jesus for later disciples.

The presentatioin of Jesus as 'innocent martyr' is another unique example. The real tensions and suffering of Luke's audience, engaged on mission and experiencing the difficulties in adapting the message of a Jewish Jesus to a Gentile world, would enable it to identify easily with a Jesus unjustly condemned and victimised for others. Such a presentation would speak most strongly to those who had suffered, been persecuted and knew of those in their midst who had already died for the discipleship of Jesus. By implication, Jesus, Luke's 'innocent martyr', could also speak to those in our own time who suffer for what they believe or are victimised by unjust political or economic structures.

4. Luke's portrait of Jesus becomes fundamental for encouraging Gospel readers to take the political and economic world of their day seriously. For Luke, the quest for religious meaning, signalled in the Gospel prologue as the purposes for writing (1:4), can only be undertaken when politics, economics and religion are seen as aspects of the one reality, a reality which is now the arena for God's action through the ministry of Jesus.

The Jesus of Luke's Gospel, presented as wisdom figure, prophet, saviour, healer, dinner host and guest, can still speak powerfully to our lives and world.

QUESTIONS

1. As you look back over the images Luke uses for Jesus, what ones stay with you the most? How relevant are they for people today?
2. Can you suggest other images which might be more pertinent today?
3. What might help people today to encounter Jesus in a new way that would be helpful to their lives?
4. What are some of the hopeful signs that suggest people still find Jesus central to their lives?

Glossary

Alexander the Great (356-323 BCE)

Alexander continued the reign of expansion begun by his father, Philip of Macedon. Alexander imposed the Greek culture throughout the Middle East, including Asia Minor and Israel. It was this Greek (or 'hellenistic') culture that influenced Jesus of Nazareth and the writer of Luke's Gospel.

Before the Common Era (BCE)

The period of history, traditionally referred to as BC, which precedes the era common to Judaism and Christianity.

Catechesis

The formal process of education by which a disciple comes to learn about Jesus and follow him in daily living.

Christian Scriptures

A term sometimes used in preference to the New Testament. In this book, the Christian Scriptures is a specific reference relating to those writings which were written by the earliest Christian communities, and have been regarded as Scripture by the Christian community and as normative for subsequent generations of Christians. Technically speaking, it must be recognised that the Christian Scriptures also include that part of the Bible which is customarily called the Old Testament.

Common Era (CE)

That period of history, traditionally referred to as AD, common to Judaism and Christianity. This division of history into CE and BCE is one which is more sensitive to Judaism and moves away from dividing history in Christian terms.

Disciple

A follower of Jesus' teachings and way of life. The Greek word for disciple, *mathetes*, means learner or apprentice.

Elite

The upper socio-economic group of first century Jewish and Greco-Roman society. People in this group were usually the minority (about five to seven per cent) who controlled the wealth and power structures which affected everyone else.

Gentile

A person of non-Jewish origin.

Greco-Roman world/culture

Though Rome ruled Israel in the first century CE, the influence of the Greek world imposed since the time of Alexander the Great remained. (See *Alexander the Great*.)

Hebrew Bible

More commonly referred to as the Old Testament. In attempting to move away from a distinction in the Bible which might infer that the writings sacred to the Jewish people have been superseded by the New Testament, scholars are searching for a more appropriate way to describe the first part of the Bible. First Testament, Jewish Scriptures and Hebrew writings have all been used. In this book, the expression Hebrew Bible includes those scriptures sacred to the Jewish people, as well as writings which were written by Jewish communities in Greco-Roman settings (for example, in Alexandria) and which have been subsequently named in some biblical collections as the Apocrypha (e.g. 1 and 2 Esdras, Wisdom, Sirach, Baruch, Maccabees, the prayer of Manasseh, and sections of Jeremiah and Daniel).

Honour-Shame

Pivotal social values in the time of Jesus and Luke. Honour was seen as the value which people had in their own eyes interpreted for them through the regard shown them by society. Honour was a person's publicly acknowledged self-worth. Shame was regarded as essentially a positive value which implied sensitivity for one's own reputation and the opinion of others.

Jewish Scriptures

See Hebrew Bible.

Literary structure

The shape which an author gives a writing. The shape becomes obvious to the hearer or reader as the writer offers literary clues which mark off one section of the writing from another.

Miracles

Actions of Jesus which reveal the reign of God overcoming the reign of evil. These actions heal people's sickness and overcome fear of evil present in those who are possessed by unclean spirits. There are also nature miracles in which Jesus' power reveals God's presence overcoming the forces of evil found in cataclysmic events (like a storm on the lake).

Non-elite

The lower economic group of Jewish and Greco-Roman society. The people of this group are the majority (about 90-95 per cent of the population) whose sources of income is derived from agriculture. (See also *Elite*.)

Parable

A wisdom riddle of Jesus which draws on images from common life that so arrest the attention of its listener who becomes caught by its sayings and its surprise ending or twist. The parables open up unexpected possibilities for the way God is present in human affairs.

Peasant

A sociological group which comprises the non-elite sector of Jewish and Roman society. Peasants are rural people who rely on the land to provide them with crops necessary for their sustenance, income and to pay taxes to the elite of society.

Prologue

The opening unit in the overall literary structure of a piece of writing. The prologue often signals some of the key themes which will emerge in the rest of the work. In the case of the Gospel of Luke, the prologue is the first four verses which present Luke's method and purpose in writing.

Prophet

One who speaks God's word by proclaiming the action of God in the present situation. A prophet is an agent of God's word.

Purity regulations

Laws derived from the Torah which enable people to provide systems of meaning for defining what is in place and out of place in society. Purity regulations were concerned with time, place, persons, things and meals.

The Seven

A group chosen at a time of pastoral need in the early Christian community in Jerusalem (see Acts 6:1-6). The Seven were appointed by the Twelve for ministry among the Greek-speaking Christian community.

Tax collector

Collaborator with the Roman imperial authorities who gained a living by extorting more tax than was legally due. Tax collectors were considered sinners, traitors and extortionists.

Theology
The systematic reflection on life in the light of the Judeo-Christian tradition which enables the presence and action of God to be discerned.

Third Gospel
The Gospel According to Luke. Sometimes biblical commentators refer to the Gospel by its position or order in the conventional books of the New Testament. Mark's Gospel is sometimes referred to as the Second Gospel; Matthew's Gospel as the First Gospel and John's as the Fourth Gospel.

Torah
The first five books of the Jewish Bible which contain the Law of God, spoken to Moses. In these books (called also the Pentateuch) are found doctrine, law, regulations (see *purity regulations* above) and also practical rules for living. The Torah was regarded as God's revelation to the Jewish people and honoured as the most esteemed section of the Hebrew Bible. Torah in a broader sense also referred to the oral law which interpreted the written law.

The Twelve
A leadership group chosen from the larger group of Jesus' first followers ('disciples'). The number was sacred to the Jewish people and was a reminder of the twelve tribes of Israel, the basic structure of its organisation. Jesus' choice of twelve represented the renewal of Israel through the community of disciples who gathered around him (see also Lk 6:12-16). With the betrayal and defection of Judas from the Twelve, the symbolism represented through the number needed to be retained. Acts 1:15-26 offers Luke's story of this.

Word
An utterance which has two dimensions – static and dynamic. The static dimension enables communication to occur; the

dynamic dimension brings about the intention of the word's speaker. In the world of Luke, a word would be better understood as word-deed.

Further reading

Joseph Fitzmyer, *The Gospel According to Luke I-IX* and *The Gospel According to Luke X-XXIV.* Anchor Bible, Garden City, NY: Doubleday, 1981, 1985. A classic work which gives detailed analysis of every passage in Luke's Gospel.

Luke: A Gospel For People on the Journey. Adelaide: Catholic Adult Education Service, 1991. A helpful ten-session program for study groups or personal reflection developed by adult educators.

Mark Allan Powell, *What are they saying about Luke?* New York: Paulist Press, 1989. A very readable, overarching introduction of Luke's Gospel that gives the reader a sense of the major themes and concerns of the Gospel writer.

John Reilly, *Praying Luke*, St Pauls, Homebush, 1994.

Robert Tannehill. *The Narrative Unity of Luke-Acts. Volume 1.* Philadelphia: Fortress Press, 1986. A narrative approach to Luke's Gospel in a way which gives the overall literary structure and themes which emerge in the story.

The Australian Biblical Project

Trainor, Michael, *Jesus in Luke's Gospel*, St Pauls, Homebush, 1995.

Kiley, Bernadette, *Jesus in Mark's Gospel*, St Pauls, Homebush, 1995.

Habel, Norman, *God in Jeremiah*, St Pauls, Homebush, 1996.

Foulkes, Pamela, *God in Isaiah*, St Pauls, Homebush, 1996.